THE PRECIOUS PEARL
© 1986 by Nick Butterworth & Mick Inkpen

First published in the United Kingdom by Marshall Morgan & Scott, 3 Beggarwood Lane, Basingstokes, Hants. RG23 7LP, England. Published in the United States by Multnomah Press.

Printed in the U.K.

Library of Congress Cataloging-in-Publication Data

Butterworth, Nick.
  The precious pearl.

    Summary: A wealthy merchant sacrifices all his material possessions to acquire an expensive pearl in this modern day retelling of the parable (Matthew 13:45) likening the kingdom of heaven to a pearl of great price.

    1. Pearl of great price (Parable)—Juvenile literature.   [1. Pearl of great price (Parable)
2. Parables   3. Bible stories—N.T.]   I. Inkpen, Mick.   II. Title.
BT378.P4B87   1986   226'.209505   85-21765
ISBN 0-88070-145-5

88 89 90 – 10 9 8 7 6 5 4 3 2

The Precious Pearl

Nick Butterworth and Mick Inkpen

MULTNOMAH · PRESS

Portland, Oregon 97266

Here is a man who buys and
sells things.
He is called a merchant.
He has a fine fur coat and a
felt hat with a floppy feather.
It is his favourite.

The house he lives in is huge.
It has five floors and a fishpond
with a fountain in the front
garden.

The merchant has everything
he wants.
He has fifteen rooms filled
with furniture.

He has four freezers
full of food.
(And three fridges
for fizzy drinks.)

And there is more money under
his mattress than you could
ever imagine. Much more.
Yes, the merchant has everything
he wants, until . . .

One day, in a shop window, he sees
something. Something special.
It is a wonderful white pearl.

'Five hundred thousand dollars,'
says the man in the shop.
It is even more money than the
merchant has under his mattress.
But he wants that pearl more
than anything in the world.

He hurries home. He has a plan.
He sells his furniture, his fridges
and his freezers full of food.
He sells his house, his fountain
and his fishpond.

He sells his fine fur coat.
But the felt hat with the
floppy feather, he keeps.
It is his favourite.

He borrows a barrow and
bundles in the money.
Off to the shop he trundles
to buy the pearl.

Oh dear! He is still six dollars
short.
'Sell me your hat for six dollars,'
says the man in the shop.
The merchant laughs.
He hands the man his hat and
takes the pearl.

Hooray! The pearl is his at last.
Jesus says, 'God is like the
merchant's pearl.
It costs everything to know him.
But he is worth more than
anything in the world.'